THIS NOTEBOOK BELONGS TO:

IMPRESSUM

Notebook - US Passport - Journal
Copyright © 2021
1. Auflage, ISBN 9798729647897
kdp – digital publishing

IDEE UND GESTALTUNG

Silvan Kaeser
Kasimir-Pfyffer-Strasse 13
CH-6003 Lucerne, Switzerland
Kaeser@StadtHirsch.ch
StadtHirsch.ch